INVADERS AND RAIDERS

THE ANGLO-SAXONS ARE COMING!

Paul Mason

Illustrated by
Martin Bustamante

W
FRANKLIN WATTS
LONDON • SYDNEY

Franklin Watts
First published in Great Britain in 2018 by
The Watts Publishing Group

Copyright © The Watts Publishing Group 2018

Editor: Julia Bird
Illustrator: Martin Bustamante
Packaged by: Collaborate

Image Credits

p.2 tl: © Walters Art Museum/Wikimedia Commons. p.3 br: © Walters Art Museum/Wikimedia Commons. p.4 bl: © Spumador/Shutterstock.com. p.5 tl: © Arterra PL/Alamy. p.5 bl: © Walters Art Museum/Wikimedia Commons. p.7 bl: © goodcat/Shutterstock.com. p.9 tr: © HIP Ltd/Alamy. p.11 cr: © Matthias Süßen/ /CC Wikimedia. p.13 tc: © jorisvo/Shutterstock.com. p.15 cr © Geogre/PD Wikimedia Commons. p.17 cr: © Ivy Close Images/Alamy. p.19 cr: © Joana Kruse/Alamy. p.21 br: © Diane Earl/N.E.N. p.23 br: © Flik47/Shutterstock.com. p.25 tr: © Premier Photo/Shutterstock.com. p.27 cr: © Joe Dunckley/Shutterstock.com. p.28 bl: © Renata Sedmakova/Shutterstock.com. p.29 tr: © Nejron Photo/Shutterstock.com. p.29 bl: © Lebrecht Music and Arts PL/Alamy. p.32 br: © Walters Art Museum/Wikimedia Commons

978 1 4451 5690 3

Printed in China

Franklin Watts
An imprint of
Hachette Children's Group
Part of The Watts Publishing Group
Carmelite House
50 Victoria Embankment
London EC4Y 0DZ

An Hachette UK company.
www.hachette.co.uk
www.franklinwatts.co.uk

MIX
Paper from
responsible sources
FSC® C104740

CONTENTS

Words in **bold** are
in the glossary
on page 30.

THE ANGLO-SAXONS

The Anglo-Saxons originally came from northern Europe. They were fierce fighters and raiders, much feared in neighbouring territories. In Britain, Anglo-Saxon raiders were a constant menace along the eastern and southern coasts.

Anglo-Saxon peoples

The Anglo-Saxons were not a single people, though they shared many beliefs and **customs**. Those who attacked Britain were mainly Angles, Saxons or Jutes. Some were Frisians and Franks. They did not act all together or at the same time. They came in waves of raiding parties led by war chiefs.

Each Anglo-Saxon group had a different homeland. Using today's place names, the Saxons, Franks and Frisians came from northern Germany and the Netherlands. The Angles were from southern Denmark and the Jutes from northern Denmark.

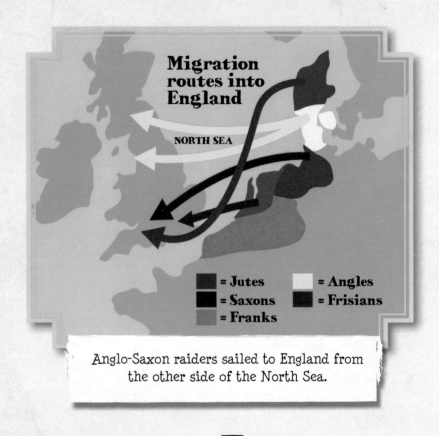

Migration routes into England

NORTH SEA

■ = Jutes □ = Angles
■ = Saxons ■ = Frisians
■ = Franks

Anglo-Saxon raiders sailed to England from the other side of the North Sea.

Forts

The Anglo-Saxons first started raiding the coasts of Britain while it was still part of the Roman Empire. The raids were so troublesome that the Romans built the 'Forts of the Saxon Shore' to defend the coast. These stretched along the shores of East Anglia and southern England.

The castle at Pevensey, on the Sussex coast, was originally built by the Romans as defence against Anglo-Saxon raiders.

Under attack

When the Roman army left in about CE 410, there was no longer one single government. Instead, local rulers took charge. Some of them came under attack from the Picts – fierce warriors from Scotland – and Celtic fighters from the west.

That wasn't all. Soon after, word began to spread. The Anglo-Saxons were coming – and this time, they were coming to stay!

The Anglo-Saxons valued precious metals and jewels. This brooch shows the skill of their craft-workers.

HOW DO WE KNOW?

How do we know what the Anglo-Saxons were like? The evidence comes from a variety of **sources.** Few from the early days are written, though hundreds of years later a book called the *Anglo-Saxon Chronicle* told the history of the Anglo-Saxons.

The Anglo-Saxons also left behind **archaeological** evidence. Their weapons, settlements, jewellery and cooking equipment, for example, all tell us about where and how they lived. Most Britons were Christians, while at first most Anglo-Saxons were **pagans**. This helps archaeologists tell whether they are looking at British or Anglo-Saxon remains.

THE ANGLO-SAXONS ARE COMING!

After the Roman rulers left Britain, we were finally free of their taxes, rules, regulations and constant bathing. Unfortunately the Roman army left too, which left us defenceless.

THE CELTS AND PICTS ATTACK

Of course, it was too much to hope that we'd be left alone. The Romans had only just gone when Celts and Picts started attacking our lands from the west and north. The stories say Picts paint themselves all over with blue plant dye, then charge into battle naked!

THE ANGLO-SAXONS ARRIVE

Next, the Anglo-Saxons started arriving. They knew the lands of Britain were rich and undefended. They've been raiding our coasts for years, and a few Anglo-Saxons had even lived here before, while they were soldiers in the Roman army.

FIGHTING FOLK

Round here, in the south-east, it was the Jutes who first started attacking our villages. Further north it's mostly Angles. To the west of here, in southern Britain, it's mainly the Saxons.

To be honest, all these people seem alike to us. They come from similar places and worship the same gods, and they're all quite keen on fighting. The differences seem to be important to them, though. That's probably why when they're not fighting us, they're fighting each other!

This tiny chapel is famous as a place where the Irish monk Saint Gildas preached Christianity.

HOW DO WE KNOW?

There are almost no records from when the Anglo-Saxons arrived in Britain. One of the few was written by a British **monk** named Gildas, probably some time in the early 500s. It is called *On The Ruin And Conquest Of Britain*.

The book tells readers about Roman Britain and the Anglo-Saxon invasion. It is not complimentary about Gildas' fellow Britons:

*'Britain has priests, but they are fools; numerous ministers, but they are shameless; **clerics**, but they are **wily plunderers**.'*

WHY ARE THEY HERE?

The Anglo-Saxons seem to have come to Britain for lots of different reasons. One story even claims that one of Britain's many kings invited them!

VORTIGERN'S MISTAKE

The story goes that this particular king, Vortigern, was worried about Pictish raiders from the north invading. He offered to pay two Jutish war chiefs, Hengist and Horsa, to fight the Picts. Vortigern's plan was for them to leave Britain once the Picts had been defeated – but it didn't work out like that.

BETRAYED

At a meeting with Vortigern and his nobles, the Jutes pulled out knives they had hidden in their shoes and killed most of the Britons. Then they seized Vortigern's kingdom. This **land grab** gave the Anglo-Saxons their first foothold of territory in Britain.

FLOODED HOMELANDS

Apparently there's another reason why more and more Anglo-Saxons are coming here. Their homelands are very close to the sea. The sea is higher now than centuries ago, and their lands keep being flooded by seawater, making them impossible to farm.

PEACEFUL INVADERS

Quite a few of the most recent Anglo-Saxon arrivals have really just come here to farm. Some have tried to settle peacefully, clearing land and building new villages – though they will always fight if they have to.

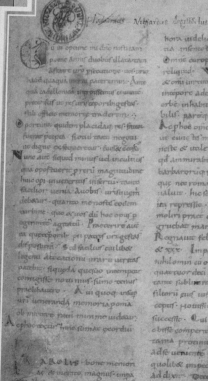

The first page of *History of the Britons*, which tells the story of when Anglo-Saxon invaders first arrived in Britain.

HOW DO WE KNOW?

The story of the massacre of Vortigern's nobles is told in a book called *History of the Britons*:

'The Saxons, speaking in a friendly way, meanwhile were thinking in a wolvish way… Hengist [gave the signal], and all the three hundred elders of King Vortigern were slaughtered, and only [Vortigern] was imprisoned, and was chained, and he gave to them many regions for the ransom of his [life].'

History of the Britons was written in the early 800s, hundreds of years after the Saxons arrived. No one knows for sure if the story is true or not.

ANGLO-SAXON SHIPS

The Anglo-Saxons haven't invaded this particular area yet, but the sight of an Anglo-Saxon raiding ship strikes terror in all our hearts.

OAR-POWERED CRAFT

The raiding ships don't have a mast and sail: they are powered by oars. Imagine how exhausting their journey from the other side of the North Sea must have been! These ships are great in a fight. Their movements are not affected by the wind, and they can turn around and change speed very quickly.

RIVER RAIDERS

What Anglo-Saxon ships are perfectly designed for is sneaking up rivers, carrying the raiders to unsuspecting villages. The ships are long and slim, and can travel in quite shallow water. That means an Anglo-Saxon raiding party can suddenly appear at almost any village within striking distance of a river.

FAST GETAWAY

Successful Anglo-Saxon raids depend on surprise and speed – the fighters arrive, grab what they can and leave before a large force can **counterattack**.

Before a raid starts, the ship is made ready for a fast getaway. It can be rowed with either end forward, so even though the ships are too long to turn around in a narrow river, they can still be rowed back to sea at high speed.

HOW DO WE KNOW?

Archaeologists have found the remains of several ships from the Anglo-Saxon era. The ships were wooden, so normally would not have survived. But they were buried in a peat bog and, in the bog's oxygen-free soil, the wood did not rot.

One of the ways we know how Anglo-Saxon ships worked is through 'experimental archaeology'. In this, experts build **replicas** of objects, based on actual remains that have been discovered. Then they use them to see if they could have worked in the way we think they did.

The Nydam boat, a 23-metre Anglo-Saxon boat made of oak, was discovered in Denmark in the 1860s. It was buried some time around CE 310-320.

FEARSOME RAIDERS

An Anglo-Saxon raider is a truly fearsome sight. This is especially true when he's charging out of the woods and all you're armed with is a basket of hen's eggs!

WEAPONS AND ARMOUR

Raiders can be heavily armed. A few will be wearing chainmail and waving a sword. Those are expensive – to have them a raider must be:

- a successful raider (= good at killing) or
- a thane (= a warrior leader who is good at killing).

Axes are cheaper than swords, but an axe with a strong **haft** is a good weapon, so you are likely to see these being waved around by raiding parties.

A few raiders wear chainmail, but a thick leather **jerkin** is the best protection ordinary raiders can afford.

Most raiders carry a spear. They have different kinds of spear for hand-to-hand fighting and for throwing.

Most raiders wear a helmet, often with extra sections to protect their nose, ears and neck.

Their wooden shields may be painted.

Almost every raider carries a long knife called a *seax*, which has one edge and can be almost as long as a sword.

HOW DO WE KNOW?

We know a lot about Anglo-Saxon weapons, partly because during battles, the metal parts of spears, axes and arrows became buried in the soil. Hundreds of years later they were uncovered by archaeologists.

The Anglo-Saxons also often buried dead warriors alongside their weapons. Great leaders would be buried with a lot of possessions – weapons, gold and silver jewellery, and other precious items that the Anglo-Saxons believed would help them in the **afterlife**.

Some of our information comes from images of the Anglo-Saxons such as the Bayeaux Tapestry (above). If the weapons the tapestry shows are similar to archaeological discoveries, the images are likely to be accurate.

ANGLO-SAXON ARMIES

Anglo-Saxon raiders mostly arrive in small groups, which hit and run quickly. When the Anglo-Saxons decide to invade instead of raid, they gather together a bigger force.

Anglo-Saxon armies are not huge. They are usually a few hundred warriors at most. Fortunately for them, they rarely have to face more than a few hundred of our men in battle.

TEMPORARY ARMIES

Like us Britons, the Anglo-Saxons don't really have big permanent armies. They gather together men for a particular aim, such as defeating another leader and grabbing his territory.

Then the surviving warriors go home as quickly as possible and get back to work in the fields.

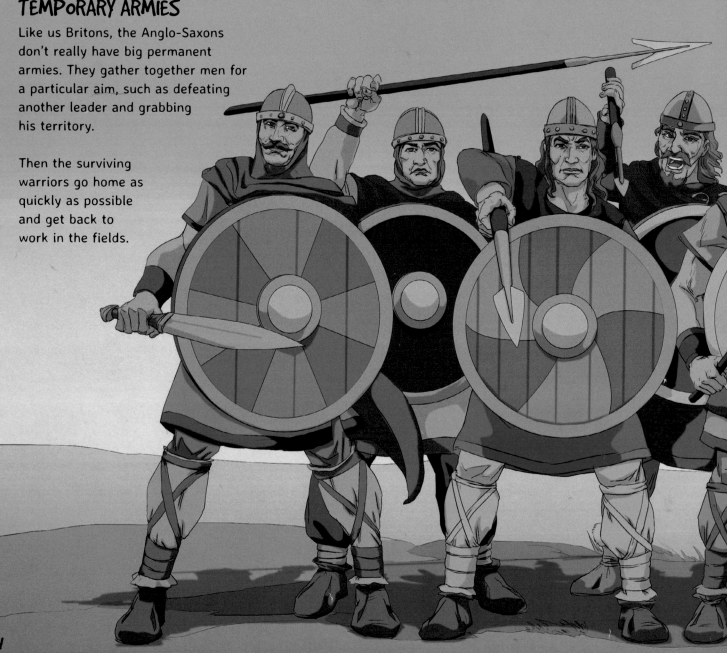

BATTLE TACTICS

A battle with an Anglo-Saxon army is basically a shoving match between two teams armed with pointy, sharp-edged weapons. One side attacks the other's **shield wall** and tries to push through it to make a gap. The other side does the same thing. All the time spears are being jabbed at you, and axes and swords are being whirled around.

ÉLITE FIGHTERS

Some of the most important Anglo-Saxon leaders always have a small group of well-trained warriors with them. These are their best fighters and are at the front of every battle. They sometimes attack the enemy in an arrowhead formation, with a few men at the front and more behind. Stopping them driving through your shield wall is almost impossible.

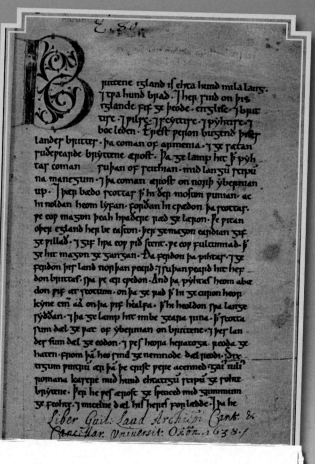

The *Anglo-Saxon Chronicle* contains the laws of Ine, which describe how Anglo-Saxon leaders raised armies.

HOW DO WE KNOW?

There is little evidence for exactly how Anglo-Saxon armies were gathered for the invasion of Britain. We do know that later, Anglo-Saxon kings demanded local leaders send them fighting men.

The punishment for not sending fighters was severe – the laws of King Ine of Wessex (an Anglo-Saxon who ruled CE 688-726) said:

'If a nobleman who holds land neglects military service, he shall pay 120 shillings and **forfeit** *his land... a commoner shall pay a fine of 30 shillings.'*

LEADERS AND FOLLOWERS

Most new bands of Anglo-Saxons that arrive here in Britain are led by a war chief. War chiefs are the most important leaders in an ordinary Anglo-Saxon's life.

THANES

Many of the war chiefs are thanes. These are important men, who have warriors who will follow them into a fight. A thane lives in a large hall and is all-powerful in his home village: he can even force another villager to leave.

CYNINGS

If a thane becomes really powerful, by defeating other war chiefs or forcing them to follow him, he might start to call himself a *cyning*, or king. There are many Anglo-Saxon kings. They're always fighting each other to get more land and power.

SLAVES

At the bottom of Anglo-Saxon communities are the **slaves**. Slaves have no rights at all and are forced to work for nothing. They work hard, sleep with the animals and rarely live for long. If the Anglo-Saxons capture you and take you back to their territory, you are almost certain to be made into a slave.

CEORLS

Most ordinary Anglo-Saxons are *ceorls*. They are usually quite poor and they live in small, simple huts. Most ceorls are farmers, but some are craftspeople, such as metalworkers, carpenters or weavers. But if their king or thane decides he's going to war, the ceorls have to stop what they are doing to go and fight alongside him.

Beowulf tells the story of a great Anglo-Saxon warrior who fights many foes, including a fiery dragon.

HOW DO WE KNOW?

Beowulf is an **epic** set in Scandinavia, but written by an Anglo-Saxon. It tells the story of a legendary warrior who – after winning numerous fights and battles – becomes king of the Geat tribe.

Like many real-life Anglo-Saxons, Beowulf becomes king because of his tremendous fighting skill. His story shows how important fighting ability was if you wanted to get ahead in the Anglo-Saxon world.

AN ANGLO-SAXON VILLAGE

Anglo-Saxons are now settling in the areas of Britain they have conquered, building villages of their own. Most of their villages are found near a river for water, and to make it easier to travel by ship.

INSIDE THE VILLAGE

The biggest hall in the village is the home of the thane and his household. There are other, smaller buildings for families.

Whatever size their home, everyone lives in a single room, where they cook, sleep and relax. The buildings have wooden walls and thatched roofs. Land is shared among the villagers and everyone has their own piece to farm.

ANGLO-SAXON FOOD

The food Anglo-Saxons eat is very simple. Their basic food is a vegetable stew: they grow cabbages, leeks, peas and carrots. In a hard year, when food is scarce, the stew might have stinging nettles or even twigs in it. That's true in a British village, too!

HUNTING

People keep sheep for meat and for their wool. Everyone wears wool clothes, as well as animal skins if it's cold. Other meat comes from hunting. Trained hawks catch pigeons. In the forests are boar or deer, but hunters who go after them have to watch out for wolves – especially in winter, when the packs are hungry and bold.

FENCED OFF

Anglo-Saxon villages usually have a wooden fence around them for defence. It keeps out wild animals from the forest and slows down any attacking enemies.

At West Stow Anglo-Saxon Village you can get a glimpse of what it was like to live in Anglo-Saxon England.

HOW DO WE KNOW?

Archaeologists have discovered the remains of many Anglo-Saxon villages in England. These discoveries tells us how the villages were usually laid out and how many buildings there were.

In West Stow, Suffolk, experts have recreated an entire Anglo-Saxon village on its original site. The wooden houses were built using the same techniques and materials as the Anglo-Saxons used.

GODS AND OTHER CREATURES

Here in Britain we'd really only just got used to the Roman gods and goddesses. Now the Anglo-Saxons have arrived with a load of new ones!

GODS AND MYTHICAL CREATURES

The main Anglo-Saxon god we hear about is Tiw, one of their gods of war and fighting. The others they're all very keen on are Woden, king of the gods, and his wife Frige.

ANGLO-SAXON GODS AND GODDESSES

STRANGE SUPERSTITIONS

The Anglo-Saxons didn't only bring new gods from their homelands. They also brought beliefs in other strange creatures: evil elves, water spirits, **ettins** and dragons. One thing you notice about Anglo-Saxons straight away is how superstitious they are. Almost everyone carries a lucky charm for protection from evil spirits and bad luck.

FRIGE

Goddess of the home
Frige is Woden's wife. She is one of the most powerful goddesses and is said to be very wise.

WODEN

Ruler of the gods
Woden is said to be the god of war, as well as learning, poetry and magic.

TIW

God of fighting
Tiw has only one hand, his left. Legend says the other was bitten off by a great wolf, Fenrir.

THUNOR

God of thunder
Thunor's favourite weapon is his hammer, and he travels about in a chariot drawn by goats.

EOSTRE

Goddess of spring
Eostre gives her name to the springtime festival we now call Easter.

WAYLAND

God of metalwork
The Anglo-Saxons valued good metalwork, so Wayland was an important god.

HOW DO WE KNOW?

We learn about the Anglo-Saxon gods and goddesses from stone carvings and written material. There are also reminders of their gods in the language we speak. Four gave their names to days of the week:

Tiw – Tuesday   **Thunor** – Thursday

Woden – Wednesday   **Frige** – Friday

There is also evidence of the gods in some place names. For example, Woodnesborough in Kent got its name from Woden, Thundersley in Essex from Thunor and Tuesley in Surrey from Tiw.

This figure of the god Tiw was discovered among the Sutton Hoo burial mound. (see page 23).

DEATH AND THE AFTERLIFE

The Anglo-Saxons take death and what happens afterwards very seriously. No wonder! There's a lot of death around if you're an Anglo-Saxon warrior.

FUNERALS

When an Anglo-Saxon dies, their funeral is an important event. The most powerful, richest people get bigger funerals. But whatever someone's rank, their funeral has to send them to the afterlife properly equipped.

PYRES AND BURIALS

Most Anglo-Saxon bodies are burned on a funeral **pyre**. Then their ashes are collected together and put into an urn. The urn is buried with important objects from the person's life, which they will need in the afterlife. A warrior is buried with his weapons, a wife with her jewellery. Some Anglo-Saxons are simply buried, without being burned on a pyre first.

DEATH OF A KING

When one of their kings dies, the Anglo-Saxons hold huge funerals. The king is buried with a great deal of treasure: jewellery, weapons and other items to show how important he was. Some of the greatest kings are buried inside a ship! We even hear that some of the king's servants are killed too, so that they can accompany the king to serve him in the afterlife.

HOW DO WE KNOW?

Many Anglo-Saxon burial sites have been uncovered. They gives clues about what people believed in Anglo-Saxon times. For example, burying someone with their most treasured possessions probably shows that these belongings would be important in the afterlife.

The greatest burial site of all was found at Sutton Hoo in Suffolk in 1939. It includes the burial mounds of about 18 Anglo-Saxon kings of East Anglia. Known as the Wuffingas, these kings claimed to be descendants of the god Woden. One mound had an entire 27-m-long ship and many treasures inside.

In 2009, another dead king's burial site was uncovered in Hammerwich, Staffordshire. It contained the largest collection of gold and silver Anglo-Saxon metalwork ever found. The collection is now called the Staffordshire Hoard.

A replica of the beautiful warrior's helmet found among the treasures at Sutton Hoo, in Suffolk.

23

CRIME AND PUNISHMENT

In Anglo-Saxon territory, someone accused of a crime has to get witnesses to say he or she didn't do it. If there are not enough witnesses, the thane decides on a punishment.

PUNISHMENTS

Many crimes are punished with a fine. For breaking into someone's house, for example, you would be fined 25 pennies, which you pay to the householder. That's a lot of money for an ordinary person! The alternatives to being fined are more serious. You might have your nose or a hand cut off, or be made a slave. For serious crimes the punishment is likely to be death.

FEUDS AND WERGILD

Anglo-Saxons often seem to settle arguments by fighting, but attacking someone can easily lead to a **blood feud** between your family and theirs. These feuds can result in nearly everyone from both families being killed. To stop that happening, the Anglo-Saxons have a system called *wergild*. If you injure or kill someone, you pay them or their family wergild.

How much wergild you pay depends on the injury and who you have hurt. For killing a thane the price is 6,000 pennies. No ordinary person could afford this, so they would be executed instead. For killing a king, it's 90,000 pennies. Only another king would be able to pay that.

This statue of Ethelbert, Anglo-Saxon King of Kent CE 589–616, is outside Canterbury Cathedral.

HOW DO WE KNOW?

There are very few sources of information about crime and punishment among early Anglo-Saxon settlers. Later, though, Anglo-Saxon kings began to record their laws, including how much wergild should be paid for particular crimes.

These wergilds were set out by Ethelbert, King of Kent, in CE 603:

Broken arm	30 pennies
Big toe cut off	50 pennies
Broken thigh	60 pennies
Fingers cut off	20-65 pennies, depending on the finger
Thumb cut off	100 pennies
Foot cut off	250 pennies
Eye removed	250 pennies

THE BATTLE OF BADON HILL

The Anglo-Saxons have been invading British territory for long enough! Our leaders decided to do something about it. They fought the Anglo-Saxons at a great, decisive battle at a place called Badon Hill.

THE BRITISH FIGHT BACK

Britons who wanted to fight back against the Anglo-Saxons gathered around a great leader. Some say he is Ambrosius Aurelianus, the last true Roman in Britain. Others claim he is a British warrior named Arthur. Whatever the truth, he gathered together a mighty army to battle the invaders.

A FINAL BATTLE

Badon Hill was actually the last in a series of battles with the Anglo-Saxons. The fighting had already roamed across southern Britain. First one side won, then the other gained a victory. Finally, the two sides met at Badon Hill, an ancient fort somewhere in the south-west of Britain.

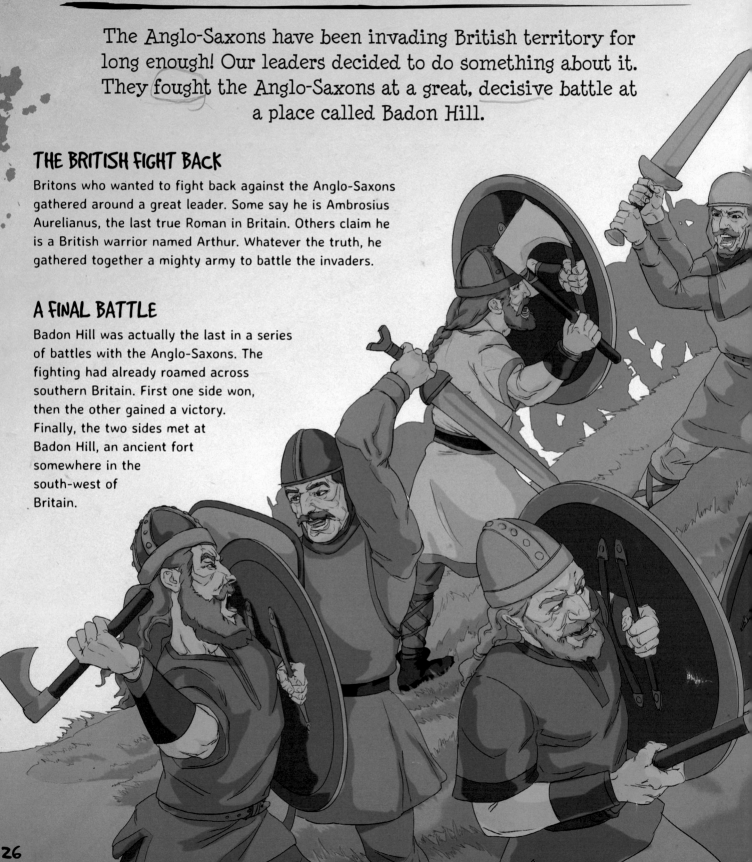

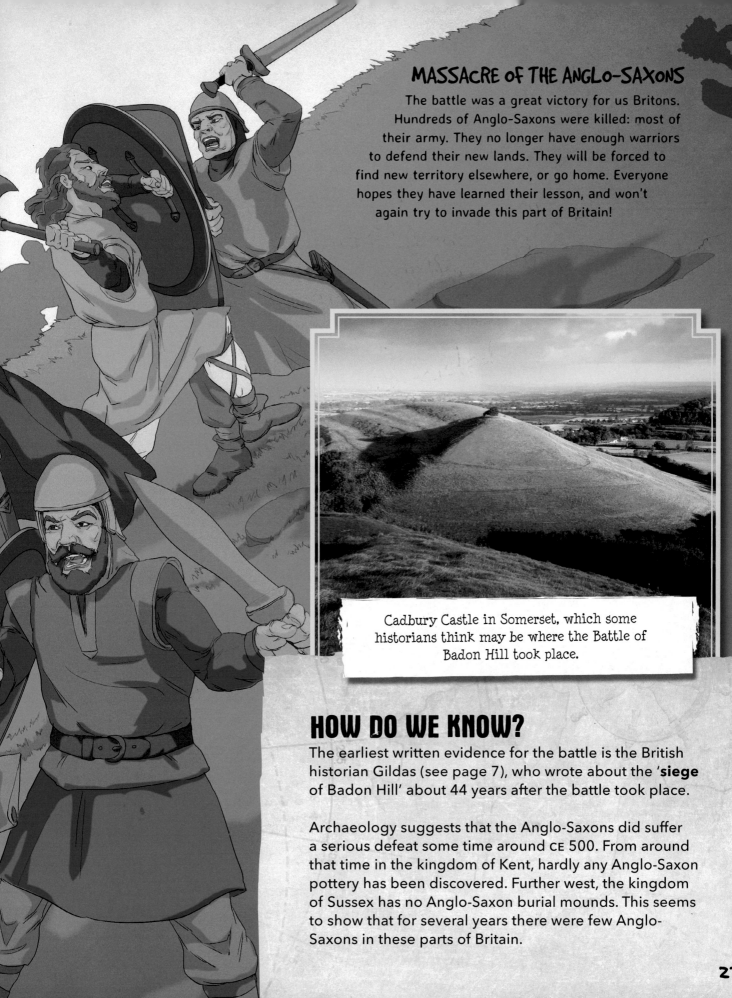

MASSACRE OF THE ANGLO-SAXONS

The battle was a great victory for us Britons. Hundreds of Anglo-Saxons were killed: most of their army. They no longer have enough warriors to defend their new lands. They will be forced to find new territory elsewhere, or go home. Everyone hopes they have learned their lesson, and won't again try to invade this part of Britain!

Cadbury Castle in Somerset, which some historians think may be where the Battle of Badon Hill took place.

HOW DO WE KNOW?

The earliest written evidence for the battle is the British historian Gildas (see page 7), who wrote about the '**siege of Badon Hill**' about 44 years after the battle took place.

Archaeology suggests that the Anglo-Saxons did suffer a serious defeat some time around CE 500. From around that time in the kingdom of Kent, hardly any Anglo-Saxon pottery has been discovered. Further west, the kingdom of Sussex has no Anglo-Saxon burial mounds. This seems to show that for several years there were few Anglo-Saxons in these parts of Britain.

RISE AND FALL OF THE ANGLO-SAXONS

Despite the defeat at Badon Hill, by about CE 600 the Anglo-Saxons occupied large areas of Britain. They took control and introduced Anglo-Saxon customs and laws.

The Anglo-Saxon kingdoms

The greatest Anglo-Saxon leaders became kings who ruled large areas of land. By the early 600s, what we now call England had taken shape. In fact, England's name comes from the **Old English** words *Engla land*, which meant 'land of the Angles'. At this time England was made up of seven main Anglo-Saxon kingdoms, though some of these later merged.

The seven Anglo-Saxon kingdoms, which today form the basis of the country we call England.

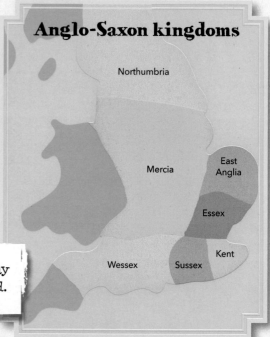

Anglo-Saxon kingdoms

Northumbria

Mercia

East Anglia

Essex

Kent

Wessex

Sussex

Christianity

In 597, a monk named Augustine arrived in Kent. His aim was to persuade the Anglo-Saxon king there to become Christian. Augustine was successful and Christianity began to spread across Britain. Eventually many Anglo-Saxons became Christians – though they may not have been that strict. In his book *History of the English Church and People*, a monk called Bede says most Anglo-Saxons are lazy Christians who are still a bit pagan!

A wall painting of Saint Augustine. He is famous throughout the Christian world for spreading his religion to new places.

The Vikings invade

From about CE 789, Viking raiders began to attack coastal settlements in Britain. In the end the Viking raiders began to settle down and form communities, just like the Anglo-Saxons hundreds of years before.

The Vikings conquer

Eventually the Vikings occupied large parts of northern and eastern England. They were beaten back by King Alfred of Wessex, but a Viking king did later take control of the whole country.

In the end both Vikings and Anglo-Saxons lost all chance of power, when England was invaded by the **Normans** under William the Conqueror in 1066.

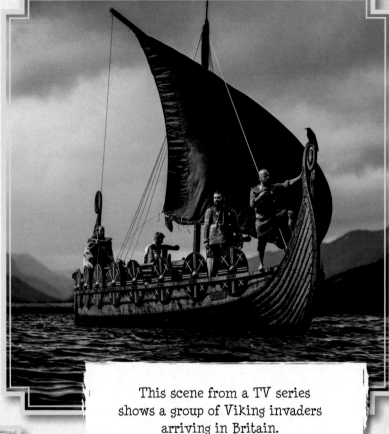

This scene from a TV series shows a group of Viking invaders arriving in Britain.

Anglo-Saxon scholar Bede (c. CE 673-735) at work on one of his books.

HOW DO WE KNOW?

Bede's *History of the English Church and People* is one of our most important sources of information about the Anglo-Saxons in Britain.

Bede wrote his book in about CE 731, roughly 300 years after the Anglo-Saxons first began to settle in Britain. He based it on a variety of sources from earlier times.

GLOSSARY

afterlife — place a person's spirit is thought to go after their body has died

archaeology — study of actual objects from ancient times

Bayeux Tapestry — long piece of cloth showing scenes from the Norman invasion of Britain in 1066 (see page 29)

blood feud — violent argument that goes on between two families for a long time

cleric — a religious leader

counterattack — attack in response to one against you

customs — the traditions and ways of life of a group of people

epic — long poem, especially one based on traditional stories

ettin — large, mythical creature that plays tricks on humans

forfeit — give up

haft — wooden handle of an axe, spear or knife

jerkin — sleeveless jacket, usually made of leather and quite long

land grab — taking control of an area of land by force

monk — member of an all-male religious order

Normans — people from an area of northern France called Normandy. In the 1000s and 1100s Norman forces invaded England, Ireland and other territories

Old English — language spoken by the Anglo-Saxons until about 1150

pagan — non-Christian (this is what the word meant in Anglo-Saxon times, today it has a different meaning)

plunderer — a person who steals goods

pyre — pile of material that will burn well, which can be used to burn a dead body

replica — exact copy of something

shield wall — line of overlapping shields that makes a defensive barrier

siege — situation where a military force inside a stronghold is surrounded by the enemy

slave — person whose freedom has been taken away and who is forced to work without payment

source — place something comes from, especially information

wily — clever and secretive

Anglo-Saxon insult contests

Although they often used fighting as a way of arguing with each other, the Anglo-Saxons also used something far less deadly: *flyting*. This involved swapping insults in verse until one side ran out of rude things to say. Among the worst things you could be called were:

a nithing – a pitiful coward

a mare – a female horse (calling a man a mare would be likely to get you killed)

Timeline of the Anglo-Saxons

CE 410

The Roman Army leaves Britain. The Britons are soon attacked along the eastern and southern shores by Anglo-Saxon raiders from across the North Sea.

MID-400s

Larger groups of Anglo-Saxons begin to land in British territory, planning to claim land for themselves. They have become invaders, rather than raiders.

ABOUT 500

A series of battles between Britons and Anglo-Saxons ends with the Battle of Badon Hill. The Anglo-Saxons are defeated and retreat.

FINDING OUT MORE

Places to visit

There are many places you can visit to see objects from the Anglo-Saxon era. Here are just a few:

The British Museum owns many objects from the time of the Anglo-Saxons, and is a great place to see old helmets, weapons and craftwork. There is more information about the museum on its website, www.britishmuseum.org.

The website section on Anglo-Saxons and Vikings for teachers and schoolchildren can be found here: tinyurl.com/cdunho2.

At the **Ashmolean Museum** in Oxford you can see many of the objects found by archaeologists in the British Isles. The museum has lots of Anglo-Saxon objects, including beautiful jewellery, glass bowls, coins and weapons. You can find out more at britisharchaeology.ashmus.ox.ac.uk.

In Suffolk are two great Anglo-Saxon experiences: the **Sutton Hoo burial site** featured on page 23 (nationaltrust.org.uk/sutton-hoo) and the **West Stow Anglo-Saxon Village** mentioned on page 19 (weststow.org).

The Offa's Dyke Centre (offasdyke.org.uk) is a great place to find out about the dyke. It is a barrier between England and Wales, built in the 700s on the orders of the Anglo-Saxon King Offa of Mercia.

Books to read

Tracking Down the Anglo-Saxons in Britain
Moira Butterfield (Franklin Watts, 2013)

Where can you see the evidence the Anglo-Saxons left behind? And how do we interpret this evidence to work out what Anglo-Saxon life was like? This book tells you the answers.

Explore! Anglo-Saxons
Jane Bingham (Wayland, 2017)

If you want to know what England was like once the Anglo-Saxons had taken over, this is a great place to find out. From Anglo-Saxon feasts to music, poetry and crafts, this book helps you to imagine what life must have been like as an Anglo-Saxon.

The Best (And Worst) Jobs in Anglo-Saxon and Viking Times Clive Gifford (Wayland, 2017)

This book is a great introduction to the kinds of jobs people did in Anglo-Saxon and Viking Britain. From an egg collector to a jewellery-maker, this is the place to find out what kind of Anglo-Saxon job you would have wanted to apply for.

Beowulf Michael Morpurgo (Walker Books, 2013)

A retelling of the Anglo-Saxon story of the adventures of the great warrior Beowulf (mentioned on page 17).

500s
Anglo-Saxons continue to raid and invade, taking control of increasing areas of British territory.

LATE 500s
The territory of the Britons is split between seven Anglo-Saxon kingdoms, known as the Heptarchy: East Anglia, Essex, Kent, Mercia, Northumbria, Sussex and Wessex.

789
The first recorded Viking attack, on Portland in the Kingdom of Wessex, signals the arrival of a new group of raiders and invaders.

INDEX